SOUL

Jacqueline Kademian

ISBN: 978-1987415131
ISBN-13: 1987415132

DEDICATION

This book is dedicated to you. May you find the ultimate soul healing on your journey.

CONTENTS

ACKNOWLEDGMENTS

I want to thank the beautiful souls who have helped me write this book. To my loved ones and clients', thank you!

INTRODUCTION

Welcome!

I am so excited to have you here for this one of a kind journal experience. Soul Therapy is an intimate journal experience like no other. It's soul work on so many levels. It's the beginning of your journey towards soul searching, self reflection, positivity and motivation.

My name is Jacqueline, and I am the creator of Positive Soul. I'm a Licensed Marriage & Family Therapist, Author and Entrepreneur. With over 7 years of experience providing therapy, I have personally witnessed the benefits of soul work, especially in journaling. I have personally gone through the process myself, and I am so grateful to have the opportunity to share my passion with you.

Through my many years of providing therapy, I have seen one major thing in common; all of us are looking for the answers within. No one has the answers but you. No one can do the work for you, but you. The secret to a happy and fulfilled life starts from within. This is the mantra I carry in all aspects of my work, and it is the inspiration for this work.

My work with thousands of clients' has taught me that we all have much more in common than we think. We are all looking for our soul answers and reflections. We want to go deeper with ourselves. We want to experience the ultimate joy in life. We want to feel the best that we can feel.

Getting to know ourselves is a difficult and challenging process. It's scary. It's vulnerability to a new level. It's also healing on so many levels.

My work in this field has inspired me to create this journal. For one year, I had an idea to prepare a project like this, but it never came to me. It was difficult to pinpoint what kind of journal I wanted to create. The inspiration was there, but my intuition wasn't guiding me to create it yet. So, I let it go for the time being, as I knew that in the right moment the idea would come back to me, if it was meant to be.

I let the idea go for quite some time, a year to be exact. It didn't cross my mind much. Then, a few months ago, the idea came back. This time, it was different. My intuition was highly involved. What seemed so difficult a year ago flowed in and was presented to me in a clear picture. Suddenly, I knew exactly what I wanted to have this journal be about.

The name also came to me out of nowhere. Before I knew it, the ideas started to flow out of me, and I followed my inner guidance to create this wonderful journal for you.

With that being said, I have been guided to create this journal for you from my inner guidance. It has flowed out of me through Source. This is exactly why I am so confident that you will receive the many benefits of this journal and really enjoy it for the next 365 days. It was meant to be created and shared with you.

This journal has been designed to be a safe space for you, where you can be fully vulnerable with yourself. There are many journals out there, but this one is different. This isn't just a journal filled with positivity, but one to be used to find your purpose and strength. Filled with prompts that will challenge you to your core, I guarantee you that this journal will be healing and revolutionary for you.

Among these pages and this 365 daily process, I hope you feel and receive the love that was poured inside.

Journaling has many benefits which will help you for the rest of your life. There are so many benefits I can go over, but I will focus on the ones I think will most help you.

For starters, this journal will get you started on the positive habit of consistency. Scientists say that it takes 21 days to begin to form a new habit. With repetitive action, you can replace negative habits or simply adopt positive ones. You will form many new habits with this journal, as the year long process is designed to evoke the habit of consistency and self discipline.

Journaling activates the mind and your thinking capacities. Taking a few moments in the day for reflection will help you stay grounded, present, and in touch with yourself. You'll be able to learn so much about yourself in this journal. You'll learn about the world. You'll learn about your life purpose and calling. You'll learn about your desires and deepest needs. You'll be faced with questions you never had to think about before.

This journal is also a present day practice of mindfulness. In psychology, mindfulness is the art of staying present and in the now. Journaling every day will allow you to be present with yourself, which will increase happiness and joy in your life. There are many mindfulness exercises in the journal as well, so you really will be getting your dose of therapy. There is a strong connection between being present and being happy.

The inspiration behind this project and one of the main benefits you will receive is healing. Journaling is extremely healing, emotionally, physically and psychologically. Writing to heal has helped release stress, anxiety, and disturbances in daily life. You will find that many of the journal entries will evoke other thoughts, feelings and behaviors in you. Follow those impulses. It may be the healing you need to move forward and live your best life yet.

Lastly, this journal will evoke creativity and passion from you. You will find your creative juices flowing. You will feel so much more aligned with your creativity and passions. You will get to answer questions and insights that will evoke strong feelings in you. You will learn so much about yourself. You'll think about things you've never thought about before.

I hope you receive the many benefits and tools in this journal. I just know that it will work miracles in your life. By the end of the 365 days, you will know yourself on a profound and deep level. You can also use these questions to get to know someone on a deeper level.

I love you, and thank you for being here. Soul therapy starts here.

How it Works

This journal is a 365 day journal, meaning that you will use it for one year. Here, I will share with you my recommendations for getting the most out of this process.

Be as consistent with the journal as much as possible. I understand that you may miss a day or not feel like doing it on some days, but the more consistent you can be, the better! You are forming an extremely positive habit with this journal, so be as consistent as you can be.

If you miss a day, it is recommended to do it the day after. Do only one journal prompt per day. It can be tempting to do more, but doing one prompt daily will help you reflect on the prompt and get the most out of it. So, even if you miss a day, don't worry, just do it the day after.

There are dates at the top of each prompt so you keep track. This way, you can start the journal at any point of the year.

You may pick the time of day which you want to do the journal prompt. It is suggested to do the prompts whenever you feel called to do so. I prefer to do them at night, as I am reflecting on my day, but you can do it at any time you feel comfortable. You don't have to do it the same time each day.

The prompts don't take long, they can literally take anywhere from a few minutes to ten minutes. It really depends on you. Don't force yourself to write a certain amount. Some days you may write a few lines, other days you will write a few paragraphs. It's not about how much you write, but what's pouring out of you that's more important.

Think of this journal as your personal diary. Be as real and honest as you can be. Remember, it's for your eyes only. The more honest you are, the more healing you will receive.

Go back and read your past prompts several times throughout the process. It will be eye-opening to see how much you have changed within the year. It will also serve as an excellent reflection of your being.

Lastly, have fun with this! Be creative. Be present. This journal will evoke creativity and passion in you. Follow your gut. Write your heart out. Enjoy the process as much as you can.

Date ________________

Gratitude for what you have will pave the way for more to be grateful for. It's important to be grateful for the small + big things each day.

Take some time today to reflect on all that you are grateful for. List them below.

Date ________________

You have about 60,000 thoughts a day. To be a positive thinker, all you need to do is make the majority of your thoughts positive.

List 10 positive thoughts that come to mind.

Date ________________

Where would you like to see yourself in 5, 10, 20 years? Write out how your life would look at each stage.

Date ________________

What is it you would like support in most?

Date ________________

Reflect upon your family. It could be a parent, sibling, grandparent or someone else.

How do they help shape your life?

Date ________________

Everyone has different needs in a relationship, what they want to give and receive. In a healthy relationship, it's important for both partners to have their needs met.

What are your needs in a healthy relationship?
How can you communicate this to your partner?

Date ___________________

Kindness makes the world a better place. Whether you are being kind to someone or someone is being kind to you, it's important to take notice of kindness gestures.

List some kindness gestures that you have done for someone or someone has done for you in the past week.

Date ________________

Travel boosts brain health and also decreases a person's risk of heart attack and depression. Going to new and different places stimulates the brain.

Where are some places you would like to travel to?

Date ________________

Harry Potter was rejected twelve times before it got picked up. Today, J.K. Rowling has a net worth that's over $1 billion dollars.

How do you handle rejection?

Date ________________

A positive role model serves as an example to lead a meaningful and positive life. Role models provide inspiration, motivation and the hope that we can all accomplish our dreams.

Who are your role models and why are they?
What are your favorite qualities about them?

Date ________________

"Life is 10% what happens to me and 90% of how I react to it." —Charles Swindoll

The way you react to what happens is more important than what happens to you. What is one experience where you can adopt a positive perception of what happened?

Date ________________

Having supportive people in your life is truly a blessing. When we feel supported, we become more confident in going after our dreams.

Who are your biggest supporters?
How do they show you support?

Date _______________

Self care is the act of taking care of your needs, being emotional, physical, spiritual and psychological needs. Taking care of yourself is a show of self love. The more you tend to your needs, the more you can take care of others.

What are your favorite self care activities?
How can you incorporate them into your daily life?

Date ________________

Make a list of 30 things that make you smile.

Date ________________

If you could ask a single person one question, and they had to answer, who and what would you ask?

Date ________________

Success has different meanings for each person. The definition of success is your own.

What does success mean to you?
What makes you feel successful?

Date _______________

Complete this sentence: "I wish I had someone with whom I could share ____________"

Date ________________

Decluttering is the act of removing unnecessary items from your environment. Having a bunch of "stuff" is a huge drain to your energy. When you hold onto many things, you are literally blocking new energy from coming into your life.

Where is one area of your environment you can commit to decluttering today/this week?

Date ________________

When was the last time you experienced so much joy and excitement, that you lost track of time?

Date ________________

The most powerful words in the Universe are the ones you tell yourself.
What you repeatedly tell yourself is what you will see manifest in your life.

What's something negative you tell yourself?
What's something loving you can tell yourself instead?

Date ________________

Breathing is extremely therapeutic. The simple act of breathing has longstanding effects. Slow, deep breathing helps calm us down. It also slows our heart rate, promotes relaxation, and helps the body rest.

Take 5 minutes to do some deep breathing exercises.
Share below how it felt.

Date ________________

How might something bad be a good thing in disguise?

Date ________________

You are the average of the people you spend the most time with. The people around you matter.

Who are the people you spend the most time with?
Do they positively or negatively impact your life?

Date ________________

"Setting goals is the first step in turning the invisible into the visible." - Tony Robbins

What are your short term goals for the next year?
What about your long term goals for the next 5 years?

Date ________________

Listening to music makes you feel calm, relaxed, and happy. Research shows that music has many health benefits, such as memory benefits, improved mood, increased happiness, lowered stress and more.

How does music make you feel?
What are the benefits listening to music has on you?

Date ________________

What are some of your favorite childhood memories?

Date ________________

If you're stuck or seemingly unable to change something, it's probably because of a limiting belief. A limiting belief is a negative thought/belief that keeps you down. It is the critical voice in your head that makes you doubt yourself.

What are some of the limiting beliefs you have?

Date ________________

Experiences are worth more than possessions. A San Francisco State University study surveyed participants and the results showed that those who focused on their experiences showed a higher satisfaction long after the moment or event passed.

What is one experience you've been wanting to do?
Can you commit to doing this in the near future?

Date ____________________

Where in the world makes you feel the happiest? Where is your safe place?

Date ________________

What's one topic you need to learn more about to help you live a more fulfilling life?

Date ________________

"Twenty years from now you will be more disappointed by the things that you didn't do than by the ones you did do, so throw off the bowlines, sail away from safe harbor, catch the trade winds in your sails. Explore, Dream, Discover." —Mark Twain

What do you want to do that you haven't done yet?
What is holding you back?

Date ________________

What does the word love mean to you? How do you show love? How do you like others to show you love?

Date ________________

The Law of Attraction states that your thoughts are always attracting. Whatever you think about will manifest in your life. The law is neutral - whatever you think about most frequently will show up in your life.

When did something you thought about manifest in your life?

Date ______________

A belief is a thought you have told yourself over and over again. Beliefs can always be changed and reframed. All you need to do is to start telling yourself a new thought.

What are some beliefs you need to let go of?

Date ________________

List 10 (or more) positive qualities you love about yourself.

Date _______________

No is a full sentence. It requires no explanation or conversation.

What do you need to say "NO" to?

Date _______________

op·ti·mis·tic
    hopeful and confident about the future

When's the last time you felt optimistic?
What can you feel optimistic about today?

Date ________________

Grounding is a technique used in therapy that helps keep someone in the present. When we are feeling stressed, we are often focusing on the past or future. Grounding helps you manage your feelings and focus in on the present.

Complete this grounding exercise;
Share 5 things you see
4 things you feel
3 things you hear
2 things you smell
1 thing you taste

Date ________________

What would you do with your life if you were suddenly awarded a billion dollars?

Date _______________

"Remember that not getting what you want is sometimes a wonderful stroke of luck."—Dalai Lama

When did not getting what you want become a blessing in disguise for you?

Date ________________

We are ruled by our habits. What negative habits do you need to let go of?

Date ________________

With action comes more confidence. Ironically, action generates more confidence and the more confident we are, the more action we take.

What action have you been holding off?

Date ________________

How can you show people you care about them?

Date ________________

Progress is achieved through small steps. Small changes add up to a big result in the long term.

What are some small steps you can take to achieve your goals?

Date ________________

What are your hobbies? Passions? Enjoyable activities?

Date ________________

To show someone you love them, are you likely to use words, actions, or another method?

Date ________________

"In nature, nothing is perfect and everything is perfect. Trees can be contorted, bent in weird ways, and they're still beautiful." - Alice Walker

How are you imperfectly perfect?

Date ________________

What is your earliest childhood memory?

Date ________________

Fill in the following;

I've been putting off ___________

Date ________________

Laughter is medicine for the soul! Laughter reduces stress, boosts your immune system, releases endorphins + so much more.

What made you laugh today?

Date _______________

If you were to make just one change in your life right now to make it better, what would it be?

Date _______________

ser-en-dipi-ty
the chance occurrence of events occurring in a beneficial way

Can you recall a moment of your life where you had serendipity?

Date ________________

When do you feel the most connected to others?

Date ________________

Your energy speaks louder than your words.

What uplifts your energy? What diminishes it?

Date ________________

"When I was 5 years old, my mother always told me that happiness was the key to life. When I went to school, they asked me what I wanted to be when I grew up. I wrote down "happy". They told me I didn't understand the assignment, and I told them they didn't understand life." —John Lennon

What does happiness mean to you?

Date ________________

True or False - "In a relationship, it's more important to be happy than to be right."

Explain your answer below.

Date ________________

Forgiveness is the act of letting go. It's releasing the past from having a hold on your future. It's not the same as forgetting or downplaying what happened. It's choosing to move on.

Who do you need to forgive in your life? What do you need to forgive them for?

Date ________________

Finish this sentence, "More than anything, before I die, I want to____________?"

Date ________________

Do you usually follow your head or your heart when making decisions?

Date _______________

Studies show that spending time outside in nature can create feelings of happiness. Nature is a natural healer; it boosts happiness, positivity, and thinking.

What are some fun activities you can start doing more of outside?

Date ________________

Is there a cause or charity you're passionate about? What does the cause mean to you?

Date ________________

How do you feel about routine? Do you have a routine or do you dislike routine?

Date ___________________

If you could go back in the past or forward into the future, which one would you pick and why?

Date ________________

The Universe rewards the decisive. The first step in getting your desire is to become clear and committed about what it is.

What do you need to commit to?

Date ________________

Reflect and write about what's on your bucket list.

Date ________________

What was your first job? What did you learn from it?

Date ________________

If you won lottery, what would you do with the money?

Date ________________

We tend to overestimate the qualities we dislike about ourselves and underestimate the qualities we like about ourselves.

How can you become more loving to yourself?

Date ________________

Make sure your choices are yours. Too many days are wasted living for someone else. When you don't follow your authentic wishes, you can grow resentful.

Do you find yourself making choices for yourself or for others?

Date ________________

If you could talk to one person in the world right now, who would it be? What would you say?

Date ________________

A self-fulfilling prophecy is when you unknowingly causes a prediction to come true, due to the simple fact that you expect it to come true. When you expect something to happen, it does.

What are some positive expectations you can have for yourself?

Date ________________

Write a letter to someone who believed in you even when you didn't believe in yourself.

Date ________________

ex·cite·ment
a feeling of great enthusiasm and eagerness

When's the last time you felt excited?

Date ________________

If you had all the money in the world at your disposal to invest in your own dream career, what kind of business would you start?

Date ________________

You are in competition with no one. The only person you are competing with is yourself.

How do you let the illusion of competition impact you?

Date ________________

You're not stuck. You have committed to certain habits because they helped you in the past. Now, those habits may be old news, harming you more than they are helping you.

What are some old harmful habits you need to let go of?

Date ________________

When's the last time you did something nice for yourself? How did that make you feel?

Date ________________

To be happier in life, judge less and accept more.

How can you let go of judgment in your life?

Date ________________

When you are feeling lost or in conflict, ask God/Universe/Higher Power for help. To receive blessings, you need to get out of your own way and be open to the answers.

What do you need to ask help for from the Universe?

Date ________________

"When one door of happiness closes, another opens, but often we look so long at the closed door that we do not see the one that has been opened for us." —Helen Keller

What comes to your mind when you read this quote?

Date ________________

Take a digital break. By mindfully stepping away from your digital devices for short periods of time, you will feel more focused and centered when you do plug back in.

How does technology impact your life? How can you be more mindful throughout the day?

Date ________________

Write a letter to someone who makes your life better. Let them know what you appreciate the most about them.

How do they positive impact your life?

Date ________________

Does spending time with other people energize you or drain you?

Date ________________

Love is the purest vibration in the Universe. When you tune into the energy of love around you, you manifest more love into your life.

Share a loving act, one someone did for you or one you did for someone else.

Date ________________

Are you taking care of yourself emotionally, physically, mentally and spiritually?

Date ________________

What's something new that you learned today?

Date ________________

Boundaries are the rules and principles you live by. They govern what you will and won't allow in your life. Your boundaries are your rules. You set them and you also have to uphold them.

How can you set better boundaries in your life?

Date ________________

Open your phone/computer and choose 3 photos of yourself across your lifetime.

How do you feel looking at your photos? How were you like back then?

Date ________________

How does it feel to be the age you currently are?

Date ________________

cre·a·tive
relating to or involving the imagination or original ideas

Are you creative? How can you be more creative in your life?

Date ________________

The words we say impact every single one of our experiences. We live and die by our tongue. We can either speak words that add to our life or detract from it.

How do you talk to yourself?

Date ________________

Ideas flow more freely when you don't have an agenda.

Process any of your thoughts below and whatever comes to your mind.

Date ________________

Don't forget to focus on the FUN in your life! Life is all about enjoying the journey.

If you could do anything fun right now, what would you be doing?

Date ________________

What would your younger self be proud of you for today?

Date ________________

Louise Hay would often do mirror work with her clients in order to promote self love. She would have her clients look in a mirror and tell themselves loving affirmations.

Look in the mirror and tell yourself,
"I love you", "I am proud of you", "You are enough"

How was this exercise for you?

Date ________________

What physical characteristics are you the most self-conscious about? How could you make peace with them?

Date ________________

What do you need from a partner? Love? Emotional support? Companionship? Soul growth?

Share why you need each quality below.

Date ________________

What's a goal you want to accomplish in the next 30 days? How can you get closer to accomplishing this goal?

Share your plan for meeting your goal below.

Date ________________

"If something you want is slow to come to you, it can be for only one reason: You are spending more time focused upon its absence than you are about its presence." - Esther & Abraham Hicks

What is absent in your life that you are focusing on?

Date _______________

We are stronger together as a community than against one another. There is enough magic in the world for us to all have what we want and accomplish amazing things.

How can you create more community in your life?

Date ________________

If you had a slogan for your life up to this point, what would it be?

Date ________________

Write about a time you failed. What did you learn about yourself?

Date ________________

Affirm these following statements and write them out as many times as you can.

I am more than enough
I completely love and accept myself
I love myself more each and every day

Date ________________

Don't chase love, money or success. Become the best version of yourself, and those things will chase you.

How can you stop chasing?

Date ________________

Visualization is mental rehearsal. You imagine images in your mind of having or doing whatever it is that you want. In a simple five-minute practice, you can use this skill to begin visualizing what you want to manifest. What you focus on expands.

In the next five minutes, visualize a goal you have for your life. Feel, taste, smell, hear what it would be like to accomplish your goal.

Share the visualization below.

Date ________________

Where do you want to live? What city and what type of residence?

Date _______________

If you could say "YES" to something right now, what would that be?

Date ________________

"You learn more from failure than from success. Don't let it stop you. Failure builds character."- Unknown

How can failure build your character?

Date ________________

If you could invent something, what would it be?

Date ________________

Who is your best friend? Write about him/her and what you love about your friendship.

Date ________________

Do you believe in fate/destiny?

Date ________________

Make a list of 30 things that make you smile.

Date ________________

mer-a-ki
to do something with soul, creativity or love; when you leave a piece of yourself in your work

When's the last time you experienced meraki?

Date ________________

What do you want to be remembered for?

Date ________________

Are you addicted to social media? How does it impact your life?

Date _______________

How does writing or journaling help you?

Date ________________

John Gottman is a relationship expert who has done extensive work with couples. He has long studied the positive and negative qualities in a relationships. He teaches that knowing the little things about your partner's life creates a strong foundation for your friendship and intimacy.

How important is it for someone to know the little things about you and for you to know the little things about them?

Date ________________

If you could snap your finger and one world problem would disappear, which one would you choose and why?

Date ________________

What's a common misconception people have about you?

Date ______________

What is something someone did that forever changed your way of thinking?

Date ________________

Second guessing yourself and being indecisive is a form of self sabotage. Learn how to trust yourself more. The decision will never be "perfect", but perfection doesn't exist. The most successful people believe in themselves and their decisions.

How have you been second guessing yourself?

Date ________________

ka-lon
beauty that is more than skin-deep

What is the most beautiful quality about you that is not skin-deep?

Date ________________

Name an animal whose characteristics you really admire.

Are you in any way like that animal?

Date ________________

Fill in the following;

My intuition speaks to me by _______________

Date ________________

If you don't like your story, rewrite it. You are the author with the pen.

Rewrite "old" stories that no longer serve you. What can you be telling yourself instead?

Date ________________

If someone were to spend an extended amount of time with you, what three things would they learn about you?

Date ________________

Mindful eating is a mindfulness exercise for reducing stress and increasing relaxation. Mindful eating helps you focus on a single sensation, which helps a racing mind.

Do you eat fast or slow? Are you present while eating? Do you enjoy your food?

Date ________________

Are you religious or spiritual? Why or why not?

Date ________________

Second guessing yourself and being indecisive is a form of self sabotage. Learn how to trust yourself more. The decision will never be "perfect", but perfection doesn't exist. The most successful people believe in themselves and their decisions, with 100% certainty.

How have you been second guessing yourself?

Date _______________

How has it felt to write in this daily journal? What have you learned about yourself in this process?

Date ________________

Celebrate! Share your success! Celebrate everything that happens in your life. No matter how big or small it is, it's important.

What can you celebrate today?

Date ________________

Write a letter to your younger self. What advice would you give yourself? What would you say?

Date ____________________

Pick five words that describe you the best and why you believe they do.

Date ________________

What's the best piece of advice a family member or friend has ever given you?

Date ________________

What's something you've always wanted to do, but worried about people judging you for it?

Date ________________

Psychologists support the benefits of affirmations. Affirmations are words and thoughts you tell yourself. All of your self-talk and your internal dialogue is a stream of affirmations.

Fill out the following affirmation with as many things that come to mind.

"I AM ____________"

Date ________________

What qualities are the most important to you in regards to a romantic partner?

Date _______________

wan·der·lust
A very strong or irresistible impulse to travel

Where do you long to go and why?

Date ________________

Life is so subtle that you barely notice yourself walking through the doors you prayed would once open.

Reflect and share about how far you have come in life.

Date ________________

What are your two most opposite personality traits? Do they complement one another?

Date _______________

Be grateful for where you are and how far you have come in life. A gratitude list can be used daily to increase your mood and positive feelings.

What are you grateful for? Share 30 things below.

Date ________________

You have the power to make others feel good about themselves, whether with a smile, compliment, or nice word.

How can you make others in your life feel good about themselves?

Date ________________

"Richness is not about what you have. It is about who you are." – Bob Proctor

Who are you? What would you answer if someone asked you this question?

Date ________________

You are being told that you will become famous tomorrow, but not what for.

What is the most realistic reason you can come up with?

Date _______________

Believing in your dreams and goals makes you a powerhouse. The more you believe that you can have what you want, the faster your goals will manifest. Have faith that what you want is coming to you, in the right time.

How can you have more faith in your goals manifesting?

Date ________________

trou-vai-lle
something lovely discovered by chance

When's the last time you discovered something lovely by chance?

Date ________________

What qualities do you look for in a close friend? Do you have those characteristics?

Date ________________

Your life can change in any instant. The miracle can happen at any time.

If you woke up tomorrow and your life was suddenly perfect, what would be different?

Date ________________

What did you want to be when you were a kid? Did your plans succeed?

Date ________________

In relationship therapy, one quality that makes a relationship stronger is the ability to continuously learn about one's partner. The deeper a relationship gets, the closer the two partners feel towards one another. The same can apply in a friendship or any other relationship.

When's the last time you really got to know someone? What did you find out about them?

Date ________________

Getting hurt is part of life. We will all get hurt in our lives. However, every person in your life has something to teach you. Even in unfavorable situations, you have something to learn from every single person.

What did you learn from the last person who hurt you?

Date ________________

Always make sure your optimistic thoughts outnumber your fears and doubts.

List 10 optimistic thoughts.

Date ________________

Do you like your job? If not, what would you like to do instead?

Date ________________

What is your purpose? Why are you here?

Date ________________

“If you hear a voice within you say "you cannot paint," then by all means paint and that voice will be silenced.” —Vincent Van Gogh

When’s the last time you silenced your inner critical voice? What did you do? How did it feel?

Date ________________

Part of developing confidence comes from stepping outside of your comfort zone. By being uncomfortable, you allow yourself to grow. The way to confidence is to habitually challenge yourself and step outside of your comfort zone.

How can you step outside of your comfort zone?

Date ________________

What is the most sentimental thing you own? What is its meaning to you?

Date _______________

Falling in love has vast effect on your body. Your body releases feel good neurotransmitters into your body, such as dopamine and serotonin, which cause feelings of excitement and ecstasy. Falling in love is a biological and emotional process, which is why it is so powerful and consuming.

Have you ever been in love? When's the last time you felt excited in love?

Date ________________

If a crystal ball could tell you the truth about yourself, your life and the future, what would you want to know?

Date ________________

What emotions are you afraid to show others? Why?

Date ________________

50% of every day life is habitual. Half of the time you are awake, you are repeating the same actions and thoughts over and over again.

What are some positive and negative habits you have?

Date ________________

vi-va-cious
full of life and good spirits

Who is the most vivacious person you know?

Date ________________

Who do you love spending time with? How do you feel when you are around them?

Date ________________

"Positive thinking is more than just a tagline. It changes the way we behave. And I firmly believe that when I am positive, it not only makes me better, but it also makes those around me better." - Harvey Mackay

How can being more positive help you and those around you?

Date _______________

How do you want people to describe you?

Date ________________

No matter what your goal is, you need to live it before you see proof of the results in your life. This can also be known as acting as if. You need to feel and experience similar features of the thing you want, in order to invite it into your life.

How can you be what you want to attract, before it comes into your life?

Date ________________

True or False - "I am able to stick up for myself."

Explain your answer.

Date _______________

We tend to overestimate how we will feel when we accomplish our goals. Research has shown that the journey is more important than the end result. When you focus on the goal alone, you forfeit the lessons and wonderful experiences that lie in the journey.

How can you enjoy your journey more? How can you be more present?

Date ________________

When did you last do something for yourself? What was it and how did it make you feel?

Date _______________

If there was a miracle tonight, how would you know it happened? How would your life look?

Date ________________

Write a letter to someone important in your life. What do you need to tell them?

Date ________________

Colonel Harland Sanders, the founder of Kentucky Fried Chicken, started his dream food chain at the age of 65. He used his first retirement social security check, $105, to start a business. He would drive around Kentucky, knocking on doors to get people to try his recipe. To date, he created one of the biggest fast food companies worldwide.

Does age hold you back from going after your dreams?

Date ________________

"You are joy, looking for a way to express. It's not just that your purpose is joy, it is that you are joy. You are love and joy and freedom and clarity expressing. Energy—frolicking and eager—that's who you are." – Abraham Hicks

Reflect upon the joy you feel in your life.

Date _______________

Music helps reduce anxiety and also helps our mind and body get through stressful times.

When has music helped you get through a difficult time?

Date ________________

What do you want your legacy to be? Are you on the path towards it?

Date 

On a scale of 1-10, how would you rate your happiness? Describe your reasoning below.

Date ________________

Who/what gets in the way of you achieving your goals?

Date _______________

Use your imagination to think about what you want to be, what you want to have and who you want to become.

Imagine everything you wanted came to you right now, how would you feel?

Date ________________

ki-lig
the rush or the inexplicable joy one feels after seeing or experiencing something romantic

What's your definition of romance? When's the last time you felt romanced?

Date ________________

How can you prioritize yourself more? What can you do?

Date ________________

"Just remember, even your worst days have only 24 hours" – *Moosa Rahat*

Reflect upon this quote, what does it mean to you?

Date ________________

Who matters most to you?

Date ________________

Time heals almost everything.

Does time heal all wounds? Has time helped you heal?

Date ________________

Comparison is the thief of all joy. Especially in our social media world, it can be easy to compare ourselves. Always remember that social media shows everyone's highlight reel. It doesn't depict the full truth.

How can you stop comparing yourself to others?

Date ________________

Describe your perfect date with a romantic partner.

Date ________________

Think like the person who you want to be like.

Who is this person and what do you think their thoughts are?

Date ________________

What are your favorite movies/shows/books?

Date ________________

"If you are in a beautiful place where you can enjoy sunrise and sunset, then you are living like a lord." - Nathan Phillips

When's the last time you enjoyed the little things in life that are often taken for granted?

Date ________________

What's more important to you – saving time or saving money?

Date ________________

The Pratfall effect is a psychological principle that explains how others will like you more if you don't come off as perfect.

Are you a perfectionist? How does that impact your relationships?

Date ________________

Who makes you feel energized/inspired? Exhausted/depleted?

Date ________________

If you had a problem, who would you go to first, your significant other, a family member or best friend?

Date ________________

Behavioral psychologists state that the way to effectively accomplish a goal is to reward yourself for progress that you make. You'll feel more motivated and excited to reach your goal.

How can you reward yourself along the way towards accomplishing a goal?

Date ________________

Do you say yes or no too much? How can you find more balance?

Date ________________

Pretend you're on a sales pitch, and the high prized item is YOU!

What are your best qualities and why would someone want to believe in you?

Date ________________

"Too many people buy things they don't need with money they don't have to impress people they don't like."
Dave Ramsey

Do you care about impressing others? When's the last time you tried to impress someone?

Date _______________

Do you easily feel guilty? What about?

Date ________________

You need to take risks in order to gain something more.
Playing it safe and staying in your comfort zone is comfortable, but unsatisfying in the long run.

How can you take more risks starting today? What will you do?

Date ________________

What repetitive thoughts and beliefs might be limiting you?

Date _______________

What makes you feel excited to get up in morning?

Date ________________

a ·dore
love and respect deeply

When's the last time you felt adored?

Date _______________

What drains your energy? What uplifts it?

Date ________________

You are in a room with a group of people who all share the same opinion on a certain topic.

Do you go with the flow or argue the counterpoint?

Date ________________

Learning about another culture will open your eyes to the world around you. Gaining an understanding of others deepens your understanding of how different people live.

What culture are you interested in finding out more about? Why?

Date ________________

If you could pick five people (anyone in the world) to be in your friends circle, who would you pick and why?

Date ________________

Imagine you were given a million dollars right now. Plan out what you would do with the money below.

Date ________________

What have you learned about yourself so far through this journal?

Date ________________

Rank the following in order from most important to least important to you.

Family
Love
Money
Work
Friendships
Travel
Material Possessions

Date ________________

You can work at a job you love for very little pay, or work at job you hate for a great salary.

Which job do you take and why?

Date ________________

Who were you closest to when you were growing up? Your mom or dad? Siblings? Grandparents? Cousins?

Date ________________

As you grow, you learn through your different life experiences. Experience is the best teacher.

What experiences have taught you the most about life?

Date ________________

Have you ever had your heart broken? How did you cope?

Date ________________

How would the people in your life describe you? What would they say about you?

Date ________________

What's something you wish you enjoyed more of as a child?

Date ________________

"We can easily forgive a child who is afraid of the dark; the real tragedy of life is when men are afraid of the light." —Plato

How might you be afraid of success? Of doing well in life?

Date _______________

If you could ask a single person one question, and they had to answer truthfully, who and what would you ask?

Date ________________

When did you not speak up, when you know you really should have?

Date ________________

Reflect upon your relationships. How would you describe the relationships in your life right now?

Date ________________

You are a guest speaker at a very exclusive convention. Millions of people will hear you speak. You have total control.

What will your speech be about?

Date ________________

Do you have a hero? Describe what you admire about them.

Date ________________

Fill in the following;

When I am in pain — physical or emotional — the kindest thing I can do for myself is __________

Date ________________

What are your top wellness tips for feeling good about yourself?

Date ________________

You are on a first date. What are the first few things you notice about your date?

Date ________________

se·ren·i·ty
the state of being calm, peaceful, and untroubled

Describe a moment you felt serene this past week.

Date ________________

What can you do today that you couldn't do a year ago?

Date ________________

Write about a compassionate way you've supported a friend recently.

How you can do the same for yourself?

Date ________________

"If not us, who? If not now, when?"
– John F. Kennedy

If not you, who?

Date ________________

Write a list of questions to which you want answers to.

Date ________________

You are at a different place today than the day you started this journal. Pick a page randomly and go back to read your response for that day. Reflect upon what you wrote.

Would your answer change if you answered that question today? Why or why not?

Date ________________

Document the moments you feel the most alive, and then rinse and repeat, over and over again.

What are you doing in those moments? How do you feel? What makes you feel alive?

Date ________________

When you think about your future, what do you fear the most?

Date ________________

Write out the top 5 limiting beliefs you carry. Cross them out, and reframe them in a positive way.

Date ________________

Make a list of everything that inspires you, from books to websites to quotes to people to stores to food to anything else you can think of.

Date ________________

Do you believe there's one person you're meant to be with? Why or why not?

Date ________________

The nature vs nurture debate within psychology is concerned with the extent to which our behavior is a product of either inherited (nature) or acquired (nurture) characteristics. There is a debate as to how much nature or nurture affects our behavior.

Do you think nature or nurture is a stronger influence on who we are?

Date ________________

"The whole secret of a successful life is to find out what is one's destiny to do, and then do it." *-Henry Ford*

What is your life purpose? Your destiny on this Earth?

Date ________________

How do you spend the majority of your free time?

Date ________________

Do not regret getting old. It's a privilege denied to many.

How can you celebrate your life more?

Date ________________

What are your five senses picking up right in this moment?

Write about the specifics - what you hear, taste, smell, see and touch. This will help you stay in the present moment and get in touch with your body.

Date ________________

Who or what do you miss in this moment? Does it feel like a sharp longing or an empty space in your heart?

Date ________________

Describe yourself in 10 words or less.

Then reflect upon this exercise, was it easy or difficult?

Date ________________

Do you believe in the afterlife?

Date ________________

Pick a supportive person in your life and text/call them to tell them how much they mean to you.

What was their reaction? How did they react? How did you feel doing it?

Date _______________

The bystander effect is a psychological phenomenon in which individuals are less likely to offer help to a victim when other people are present. The more people who are present at an emergency situation, the less likely it is that any one of them will help.

How can you step up and offer someone help?

Date ________________

What always brings tears to your eyes?

Date ________________

What's your favorite way to receive affection?

Date ________________

"You can't connect the dots looking forward; you can only connect them looking backwards. So you have to trust that the dots will somehow connect in your future. You have to trust in something--your gut, destiny, life, karma, whatever. This approach has never let me down, and it has made all the difference in my life." --*Steve Jobs*

How can you develop more trust in your future?

Date ________________

How do you feel about blind dates? Have you ever been on one? How was your experience?

Date ________________

If you could be doing anything in the world right now, what would you do?

Date _______________

Fill in the following sentence;

I feel happiest in my skin when ________

Date ________________

What are the things that really get under your skin?

Date _______________

Reflect upon a time when you worried about something and nothing happened.

Date ________________

What's been on your mind today? What have you thought the most about? Reflect and process below.

Date ________________

You partner is not giving you something you need. Do you tell them or suffer in silence?

Date _________________

Are you most comfortable with a lot of people, or do you prefer the company of few?

Date ________________

"I want to encourage women to embrace their own uniqueness. Because just like a rose is beautiful, so is a sunflower, so is a peony. I mean, all flowers are beautiful in their own way, and that's like women too." - *Miranda Kerr*

Make a list of all the women in your life and what makes each of them unique.

Date ________________

Do you get bored easily? Why do you think so?

Date _______________

If you had a friend that you spoke to the same way you speak to yourself, how long do you think that person would allow you to be your friend?

Date ________________

If you had to choose right now, would you pick fame or money? Why?

Date ________________

When did you last push the boundaries of your comfort zone?

Date ________________

How do you manage stress? What has worked for you and what hasn't?

Date _______________

If you're under tons of stress, your brain does not perform optimally. You actually perform worse. That's why it's so important to make time for self care.

When's the last time you took a break/day off?

Date ________________

Reflect upon a time in your life you felt especially valued and loved.

Date ________________

Have you accomplished anything on your bucket list? Why or why not?

Date ________________

Are you making physical and emotional space for what you want to manifest in your life?

Date ________________

“We cannot solve our problems with the same thinking we used when we created them.” - Albert Einstein

What new ways of thinking will help you solve your problem?

Date ________________

What's one thing about your life you would never change for someone else?

Date _______________

If your body could talk, what would it say?

Date ________________

Write a letter to your future self, 5 years from now. Write about your life as if you are an outsider looking in.

What do you do? What do you think about? What stresses you out? On and on.

Date ________________

Have you been able to be honest and vulnerable in this journal? How has it felt to share (or not) this much?

Date ________________

When you think of home, what immediately comes to mind?

Date ________________

Science shows how closely smell is tied to our memories. A familiar scent from the past can bring up many forgotten memories, some you forgot you had.

What smell reminds you the most of your childhood? Why?

Date ________________

Make a list of everything you'd like to say YES to right now.

Date _______________

"Happiness is an attitude. We either make ourselves miserable, or happy and strong. The amount of work is the same." – *Francesca Reigler*

How can you adopt the attitude of happiness?

Date ________________

How many people do you truly love? What are you doing for them?

Date ________________

What's surprised you the most about your life?

Date ________________

Is love scary for you? Why or why not?

Date ________________

Write a letter to your parents, anything that comes to your mind.

Date ________________

What do you love the most about your culture/heritage/ethnicity?

Date ________________

Whose life have you had the greatest impact on? What would they say about you?

Date ________________

Do you ask enough questions? How can you ask more meaningful questions in your life?

Date ________________

The Universe supports me.

I am loved and adored.

I am being guided.

I am more than enough and have so much to offer.

There is always more coming in than going out.

Which affirmation sticks out the most to you? Write it out as many times as you can.

Date ________________

When you're 90 years old, what will matter most to you in the world?

Date _______________

Write a list of questions to which you urgently need answers to.

Date ________________

What is the best gift you have ever given or received?

Date ________________

You just receive a call from your best friend and are told to pack, as you are going on a trip to a destination on your bucket list.

Do you go or is it too short notice?

Date ________________

How do you handle a bad day? What makes you feel better?

Date ________________

If you were stranded on a desert island, what is the one thing and the one person you would choose to be with you?

Date ________________

A common misconception is that our emotions affect the way we communicate. In fact, the opposite is true: the way we communicate has an influence on our mood.

How can you be more of a conscious communicator, with yourself and others?

Date ________________

"Take into account that great love and great achievement involve great risk." - Dalai Lama

When's the last time you took a risk? How did it go?

Date ________________

If you received enough money to never need to work again, would you quit your current job?

Date ________________

Who are you? Describe yourself below without using your name, or any attributes given to you by society.

Date ________________

List 20 things you are grateful for today.

Date _______________

Make a list of the people in your life who genuinely support you, and who you can genuinely trust.

How can you show your appreciation to them?

Date ________________

Choose a quote that inspires you and write what it means to you.

Date ________________

How do you maintain your physical health?

Date ___________________

What does growing older mean to you? How do you feel about it?

Date _______________

If you can't stop your stream of thoughts at night, writing them down will help calm your mind, so you can sleep.

What have you been thinking about recently? What's keeping you up? Use the space below as a free space for writing.

Date _______________

du-en-de
the mysterious power of art to deeply move a person

When's the last time you felt duende?

Date ________________

What was the funniest thing you saw or heard this week?

Date ________________

What's one secret you have kept from the people close to you?

Date ________________

Fill in the blank;

I feel amazing when _____________

Date ________________

Today, take some time to go back and reread some entries from the beginning of this journal.

What surprises you the most about what you wrote? How different are you from that person who started this journey?

Date ________________

Write about something you are looking forward to in the next few weeks or months.

Date ________________

What are your greatest strengths?

Date _______________

The present moment is all that exists. Too often, we think about the past or future. In reality, the present moment is all we have right now.

Do you find yourself looking in the past or future a lot? How can you enjoy the present moment more?

Date ________________

If you woke up tomorrow and everything in your life was perfect, what would be different?

Date ________________

What is your favorite part of your body? What do you love about it?

Date ________________

What did your last relationship teach you?

Date ________________

Celebrate your life. You have so much to celebrate. Simply being alive is a celebration, as you had only 1 in 4 quadrillion change of being here.

What can you celebrate in your life today?
What were some of your favorite celebrations in life?

Date ________________

Fill in the following;

I couldn't imagine living without ___________

Date ________________

If you could solve three problems in the world right now, which would they be and why?

Date ________________

What does an ideal weekend look like for you?

Date ________________

How would you like to grow and evolve in the following year?

Date ________________

Do you usually stay friends with your exes? Why or why not?

Date ________________

The illusion of progress is extremely motivating. According to research, if you believe that you're progressing toward a goal, you move faster toward achieving that goal.

Reflect about how you have been progressing towards your goals.

Date _______________

If your entire life up to today was a movie, what title would best fit?

Date _______________

What are relationship deal breakers for you? Why?

Date ________________

Nature is extremely therapeutic. Some of the positive effects of being out in nature include increased mood, reduced stress, improved cognitive performance and increased happiness.

How often are you in nature? Do you feel the positive effects?

Date ________________

What is your greatest weakness?

Date ________________

What does family mean to you? How important is your family in your life?

Date ________________

"Never be bullied into silence. Never allow yourself to be made a victim. Accept no one's definition of your life; define yourself." *Harvey Fierstein*

When's the last time you remained silent when you had something to say? Why did you keep quiet?

Date ________________

Have you ever lost someone close to you? What do you wish to say to them?

Date ________________

What's the one thing you would like to change about yourself?

Date ________________

If you had to pick 3 words to live by for the next month, which words would you pick? How can you bring those words to life?

Date ________________

Do you enjoy celebrating your birthday? Why or why not?

Date ________________

Studies have shown that happiness is contagious. It can be hard for people to walk away from someone who is happy. Happiness is a magnet.

List 10 things you are happy about today.

Date _______________

mu-di-ta
feeling joy on someone else's behalf

When's the last time you felt mudita?

Date ________________

What would you do if your parents didn't like your partner?

Date ________________

What do you love most about your generation? What do you dislike?

Date ________________

Would you relocate for love?

Date ________________

Write out your life story in as much detail as possible.

Date ________________

Many studies have shown that spending money on experiences rather than possessions (items, objects) yields much more happiness.

Do you believe this to be true? Why or why not?

Date ________________

What do you think the most about when you're by yourself?

Date ________________

"A man travels the world over in search of what he needs and returns home to find it." – *George Moore*

How might what you need be already inside of you?

Date ________________

Share a loving act, one someone did for you or one you did for someone else in the past week.

Date ___________________

If you could choose one superpower to have for the rest of your life, what would it be?

Date ________________

When you are feeling lost or in conflict, ask God/Universe/Higher Power for help.

What do you need to ask help for from the Universe?

Date ________________

If you are feeling stuck or lost about your passion, take some clues from your childhood. The toys and games you played with as children serve as big clues as to where your passion lies.

What toy did you love as a child? What did you love to do? Where did your imagination take you?

Date ________________

Which phase of your life was the most eye-opening and life changing?

Date ________________

You got great news today that you can't wait to share.

Who do you tell first: Your best friend, your partner, your family, or social media?

Date ________________

If you could talk to your teenage self, what would you say?

Date ________________

Which book has touched you on a personal level. Why?

Date ________________

Reflect about how you have changed in the past five years.

What's so different about you? What have you learned?

Date ________________

"Look for good things about where you are, and in your state of appreciation, you lift all self-imposed limitations – and all limitations are self-imposed – and you free yourself for the receiving of wonderful things."
- *Abraham Hicks*

List all of the good things about your life in the present moment.

Date ________________

Your neighbors are having a party. You don't know anyone who is attending. Do you go to the party?

Date ________________

Choose a convenient mealtime and eat slowly. Focus on each sensation as you eat, such as the smell, sight, touch, sound and taste of the food.

How does it feel to eat mindfully?

Date ________________

What is going well in your life right now?

Date ________________

Fill in the following;

I feel like myself when____________

Date ________________

What are five things you value the most about yourself?

Date ________________

Having butterflies in your stomach is a real feeling, caused by an adrenaline rush! It can be hard to avoid the feeling, especially when embarking on a new adventure or falling for someone.

When's the last time you felt butterflies?

Date ________________

What would your best self, the version of yourself who has everything she wants, be thinking and doing right now?

Date ________________

How has your intuition communicated with you recently? What messages have you received?

Date ________________

Would you rather break someone's heart or have your heart broken?

Date ________________

There are two energies in our body; the masculine and feminine energies. We possess each energy to certain degrees, even though one tends to be more dominant.

Are you living more in your masculine or feminine energy? How does that impact your life?

Date ________________

"Your vision will become clear only when you can look into your own heart. Who looks outside, dreams; who looks inside, awakes." – *Carl Jung*

Have you been looking into your heart? Why or why not?

Date _______________

What were your highs and lows today?

Date _______________

What lessons are you currently learning?

Date ________________

If you could go back in time and change one thing from your past, what would it be?

Date ________________

How can you have more fun?

Date ________________

Write out a letter with the following prompt, with whatever comes to mind.

DEAR UNIVERSE,

Date ________________

What area of your life do you need the most healing in? How can you take the next steps towards healing?

Date ________________

What/who are the most beautiful people, places, and things to you?

Date ________________

List 20 things you absolutely love about yourself.

Date ________________

How has this journaling experience been for you? How has it felt to share so much of yourself, with these pages?

Date ________________

Reflect upon what you have learned about yourself from this journal.

ABOUT JACQUELINE

Jacqueline Kademian is a Licensed Marriage & Family Therapist, Author and Entrepreneur. She is the creator of the personal development brand, Positive Soul. She uses spirituality and psychology techniques to help others create massive changes in their lives. Specializing in relationships, self-love, mindset and manifestation work, she is able to help her clients' create lasting change. Jacqueline is unique with her soft-spoken, clear, and relatable teaching style. She is able to provide healing and transformation by helping her clients' find their power and greatness.

If you'd like to find out more about Jacqueline and the other products she offers, visit her on her website, https://positivesoul.net. You can also find her on Instagram, @positive___soul, where she posts inspirational content.